FELTMAKING

Color plate 1 *A rosette motif was chosen for this blanket.*

FELTMAKING

Techniques and Projects

Inge Evers

Lark Books

Asheville, North Carolina

Photography: Hans van Ommeren, the Netherlands
Design: Karel van Laar, the Netherlands
Illustrations: Ger Daniels, the Netherlands
Pattern drawings: Hetty Paerl, the Netherlands
Color plate 2 and fig. 49 and 50: Tony Lumb, England

Translated from the Dutch by Marianne Wiegman

Production, English language edition: Thom Boswell, Valerie Ward

First English language edition published in 1987 by Lark Books,
50 College Street
Asheville, North Carolina 28801

English translation © 1987 by Lark Books

10   9   8   7   6   5   4   3

First published in the Netherlands under the title
Vilt Maken
© Cantecleer bv, de Bilt 1984

Library of Congress Catalog Card Number: 87-80486

ISBN 0-937274-34-8

Printed in Hong Kong.

Contents

6

Introduction

During the last two decades there has been a revival of interest in working with felt, the oldest textile form on earth. Or, as one cheerful American remarked: "Felt is the latest hit from the past." Since the seventies, this craft "from the land of felt"* has been popular again. The excavation of ancient felt pieces was exciting news on many fronts. The technique appeared to be of special interest to scientists and museum experts as well as to artists and teachers. The interest was contagious, and very soon people in all parts of the world were making felt again. Why did this happen? There may be many different opinions. My own is that feltmaking is a craft that suits everyone—young and old, children, men and women of all ages.

I hope that by reading, looking and doing, you will become enthusiastic about feltmaking. And that you, like my pupils and I, will discover that felt lends itself to making beautiful, warm and waterproof clothing, toys and household articles, but also to intriguing experiments, to new discoveries and, finally, that you find it to be a very enjoyable activity.

I. E.

Left *This blanket is used as a wall hanging. The fans are of silk, dyed in a multicolor bath. The fan pattern was incorporated into the second layer from the top. The top layer, of wool, was cut away during the felting process to expose the fans. So the fans could be found again after the top layer was in place, a plastic negative was made from the whole pattern from which the fans were cut. The cords were spun from the same silk used for the fans.*

*Felt was so important in the lives of the Mongols and the people in Chinese and Russian Turkistan that during the Middle Ages the whole northern steppe district was known to the Chinese as "The land of felt."

I. The History of Felt

What is Felt?

Felt is a non-woven material which is created by the compression of wool, with the help of moist heat and rubbing but without the use of a binding compound. Wool is the only fiber endowed by nature with the properties which enable it to be felted. Plant fibers, artificial fibers, and animal hair also can be made into felt if mixed with wool.

The way in which wool becomes felt can be observed under a high-powered microscope (fig. 1). A wool fiber is covered with small scales. When the fibers are subjected to pressure, and are rubbed with moisture, the scales open. As this treatment continues the scales hook together and, because the wool also shrinks, form a firm, tight material.

A funny anecdote which illustrates this process is one about the son of King Solomon. He was a professional shepherd. For a long time he pondered the problem of how to make fabric from wool without having to first spin the wool into yarn, then to braid, knot or weave the yarn into fabric. One day, in his frustration, he stamped up and down on a sheepskin while crying hot tears. When his tantrum subsided he saw to his amazement that stamping his feet had worked his tears into the wool, and he was standing on felt!

Looking Back in the History of Felt

From the earliest times, the craft of feltmaking was practiced by nomadic peoples. They traveled with camels, sheep, goats, and later also with horses, over the steppe, never making permanent homes. Since prehistoric times nomads inhabited the area between the Arctic circle and the subtropics. They had to adapt continually to changing living conditions because of their dependence on nature and the surrounding environment.

Each tribe had its own culture, but in

1 *The wool fiber is covered with small scales. These scales open under pressure and when rubbed with moisture. As this treatment continues, felt is created.*

2 *Animals were always depicted symbolically: a deer, a griffin, a lion and a butterfly.*

9

the struggle for existence all the tribes used the same tools, weapons and saddlery. There also were common denominators in their art. Animals were a frequent theme; they symbolized the mighty forces of nature (the Scythian or Siberian style of animal figures are shown in fig. 2). What these people produced for daily living was, in addition to being functional, so artistic that many of those articles are now declared to be cultural treasures.

The earliest prehistoric findings date from the Neolithic period (6500-6300 B.C.). Other important excavations are from the Bronze Age and the Iron Age. The most famous of these art treasures found to date come out of the rich burial mounds in the Altai mountains of the U.S.S.R., such as those of Pazyryk. The normally perishable materials, like felt, wool fabrics, fur, and leather, were well preserved. This was caused by the way the graves were constructed to allow frost and ice to enter. Because the dead were buried with their possessions, such

as clothing, jewelry, musical instruments, horses and tack, pottery, etc., these finds give an excellent picture of the nomads' way of life and the style of their art.

Look closely at the drawings of the swan (fig. 3) and the griffin (fig. 2b), two examples of animal motifs used in felt. The three-dimensional swan worked in colored felt applique served as an adornment of a burial tent. The griffin, with its notched comb and collar, is appliqued on a white felt saddle blanket.

The largest felt work yet discovered from this period is a hanging tapestry measuring 4.5 by 6.5 meters. It is now on exhibit in the Pazyryk room of the Hermitage Museum in Leningrad. There are many mythological animals portrayed on it, and floral patterns as well. In fig. 4 you can see a detail: a rider on a horse. In the border are appliqued positive and negative forms. It is very interesting for the modern feltmaker to see how far advanced were the techniques used in this ancient tapestry. It is an inexhaustible

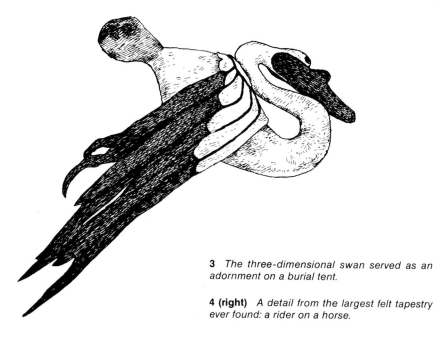

3 *The three-dimensional swan served as an adornment on a burial tent.*

4 **(right)** *A detail from the largest felt tapestry ever found: a rider on a horse.*

source of inspiration and encourages one to investigate all the possibilities of feltmaking. In addition to applique, mosaic and inlay techniques also are used, and rich embroidery accentuates the motifs.

In chapter III instructions are given for several of these techniques in felt. You can experiment with them all, and let your imagination take it from there.

Living with Felt

Felt played an important part in the nomadic life. Even their homes, large collapsible tents (fig. 5) were covered and furnished with felt. These tents are often mistakenly called "yurts." The yurt actually was the site upon which the tent stood, not the tent itself. The frame of the tent was light, portable and foldable. It was circular, conical toward the top.

The frame, a wooden criss-crossed lattice, had a diameter of 6 to 10 meters.

The rounded form helped the tent withstand strong winds. The framing was completely covered in winter with pieces of felt material. They in turn were attached to the lattice with woven bands. This provided adequate protection against cold, rain and snow.

In summer the felt walls were rolled up. The door opening always faced south. The smoke hole in the middle of the roof was left uncovered in summer and served as a sundial.

Inside the tent was a large living area which was subdivided into sections for the man and the wife of the household, the children and other family members, a place of honor for high-ranking guests, and separate places for male and female visitors (fig. 6). Servants and peasants remained at the entrance of the tent, often an extremely cold place to sit. Their space might be shared at times with the family's young livestock.

5 *Nomads needed felt for survival. Their homes were collapsible, felt-covered tents.*

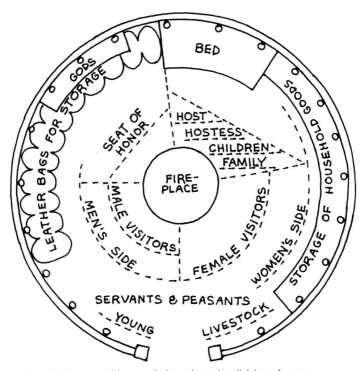

6 *Inside was a large living area with an orderly and precise division of space.*

Around the walls were leather bags for storage of food and household articles. Possessions also were kept in wooden trunks covered with felt (fig. 6a). Furniture was made exclusively from felt. Baby's cradle was a hammock of folded felt. The floor was covered with decorated felt carpets, each with its own place and meaning.

When the family wished to move on the tent could be taken down by a few people in half an hour, and carried by two camels to the next yurt (fig. 6b). To re-assemble the tent would take one to two hours.

6b *The tent was carried by two camels to the next yurt. The camel, of course, wears a saddle blanket made of felt.*

6a *Household goods were stored in felt-covered trunks.*

13

II. Basic Techniques and Equipment

Before you learn to make felt, you might check to see whether you already have the equipment you'll need. The materials you will use are listed below. On page 85 are names and addresses of suppliers who sell feltmaking materials.

For your first attempts at feltmaking, it would be wise to use batt-carded wool from New Zealand sheep. Nearly all the samples in this book were made with this kind of wool. Where another fiber is used, it is noted. The wool used here is from Romney sheep.

Once you become a bit more proficient at making felt, then you might also try the materials noted below. As a rule, anything you mix with good felting wool will also felt—even plastic and chicken feathers.

Certain sheep produce wool with especially good felting wool: Jacob, Gotland Pelssheep, the heather sheep from the Dutch province of Drente, Iceland sheep, and the Persian karakul.*

The hair of some animals also has felting properties, such as that of the camel, llama, alpaca, goat, and yak. A nicer quality of felt will be obtained when the hair is mixed with sheep's wool. Dog, cat, and even human hair can also be felted along with wool. Plant fibers, too, can become felt when mixed with wool. Flax, hemp, ramie, and cotton all are suitable. Silk combined with wool gives a nice gloss to the resulting felt. Combining of fibers will be explained in chapter III.

Useful supplies for feltmaking are (shown in fig. 7):

1 A rush mat, about 60 cm by 2 m.
2 Synthetic window screening. It is helpful to have a piece of non-fraying screen the same size as the rush mat. You can cut a few small pieces to use for making samplers. The larger pieces can then be used for a vest or boots.
3 Old towels to soak up excess soapy water.
4 Soap. Pure soap, such as olive soap or soap powder is best, not detergent.
5 Sprinkling bottle: a laundry sprinkler, or a plant mister.
6 Sturdy, pliable plastic from which to cut out patterns.
7 Washboard, rolling pin, broom handle. All these are used to "full" the felt.
8 Apron
9 Needle and thread
10 Pen and paper
11 Measuring tape (in centimeters)
12 Scale (metric)
13 Waterproof pen
14 Hand cards and/or drum carder
15 Form in which to make felt, such as a cake pan
16 Felting fibers

* The wool of particular breeds of sheep may be difficult to obtain in certain areas. In general, medium staple wools—the finer, softer wools—are best for feltmaking. In the U.S. and in Britain the wool of Merino, Romney, Corriedale, and Marsham sheep is readily available and is suitable for feltmaking. Local suppliers also can make recommendations, and a list of mail-order suppliers is given on page 85.—Ed.

Carding

One of the most important preparations for making felt of even thickness is the carding. Nomads used, among other things, the feltmaker's bow. As you can see in fig. 8, this bow resembles a musical instrument. It has one string, under

7 *The tools needed for feltmaking. Even a rolling pin has its use. Not shown, but necessary, are plastic, for patterns, and an apron.*

tension, that lies nearly horizontally 1 cm below the wool. When the string is hit with a wooden hammer it starts to vibrate. The vibrations cause the topmost layer of wool to become airy and porous. Handling the bow required a great deal of skill.

Carding on the Drum Carder

We now have more modern equipment, such as hand wool cards and the drum carder. With these, too, one must be very precise. When you feed the wool into the carder, hold your hand as closely as possible to the feeder board (fig. 9). This prevents your hand from touching the small hooks. Use a small amount of wool at a time so the mill will turn easily and the wool will divide itself evenly over the drum. Take care that the wool stays 2 cm away from the edges, otherwise wool may go into the axle and cause the carder to lock.

When you want to mix different fibers and/or different colors of wool, you can also fasten tufts of material on top of the large roller. With a little bit of practice you can make many fiber designs and color mixtures this way.

When the wool on the large roller is 1 cm thick, take it off as follows. Turn the drum so the blank area at the seam is toward the top. Put a knitting needle or a finger under the combed layer of wool at this point (fig. 11). Lift the wool to make an opening across the width of the roller. Then, with your left hand, pick up all the fibers while slowly turning the handle backward with your right hand (fig. 12). While turning, lift the carded piece higher and higher until you hold the whole piece in your left hand.

If there are still fibers on the roller, you can remove them with the small brush that comes with your carder. In this case, too, turn the wheel slowly backward while removing the wool.

The piece that you have taken off is not yet ready for felting. You still need to divide it into smaller pieces or strips (see figs. 13, 14, 15).

8 *This bow, used for carding, resembles the bow of a musical instrument.*

Carding by Hand

There are many misunderstandings about hand carding. Often the complaint is that it is such heavy work. That is indeed the case if too much wool is used at one time and if the cards are beaten together with force. The results are scraping noises, sore arms, and in addition an inadequate arrangement of the wool. Try it a few times following the directions here, and you will see that it can be pain- less, and even fun and relaxing.

1 Put the left card on your left knee. With your left hand, palm upward, hold the card so that the handle points away from you and the small hooks on the card are upward. With your right hand attach small tufts of fiber near the upper edge of the left card (fig 16).

2 Keep the left card on your left knee, with your left arm stretched out. Hold the right card with the right hand palm down- ward. Comb lightly through the fibers

9 When feeding the wool into the carder, keep your hand as tightly as possible against the feeder board.

10 To mix different fibers and/or colors of wool, you can place tufts of the contrasting material on top of the large roller.

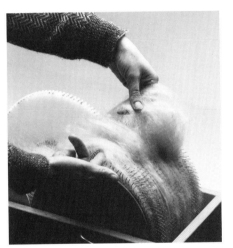

11 To remove the wool, insert a finger or knitting needle under the combed layer at the opening across the drum.

12 With your left hand, pick up all the fibers at once, while turning the handle slowly backward with your right hand.

17

13 The carded wool is divided into a continuous strip. Working with both hands, separate a strip almost to the bottom of the batt.

14 Then start the next strip, so you will have one long strip from the carded piece. To prevent tangling, wind it into a ball.

15 Divide the long strip into pieces comparable in size to those you carded by hand.

with the right card (fig. 17). Try not to let the metal hooks mesh.

3 The carded wool is transferred to the right card as follows. Turn the right hand over and hold the card on your right thigh. The left card is placed at a right

angle to the right one. With the cards in this position, use a scraping motion to take the fibers off the right card (fig. 18). Repeat the process a few times, transferring as often as necessary.

4 To remove the wool from the cards, place the cards vertically against one another with both handles pointing upward. Again place one card at a right angle to the other and transfer the fibers. Repeat this several times and the fibers will move to the top of the small hooks from which they can be loosened easily.

5 Now the wool is in a rectangular form. Place the wool carefully on a sheet of paper and cover it with a second sheet. Repeat the carding process until you have enough wool for your project.

6 Another way to remove wool from the cards is to shape it into small rolls, or rolags. Hold the cards as in step 4, with the handles upward. Keeping them in this position, move your hands upward, alternately, with short jerks. Repeat a few times and the wool will lay as a small carded roll along the top edge of the card (fig. 19).

Color plate 2a *Dyeing with steam: pouring the first color over a mixture of wool and silk.*

2b *Pouring the second color.*

2c *Pouring the third color.*

2d *There is enough dye for an exhaust bath.*

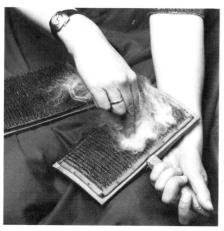

16 *Place small tufts of wool toward the top of the left card.*

17 *Comb lightly through the fibers with the right card. Don't let the teeth mesh.*

18 *Transfer the wool from one card to the other. Note the position of the hands: cards upward, palms upward.*

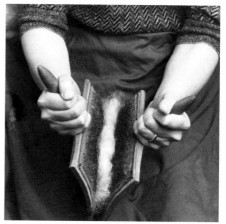

19 *Making a small roll, a rolag. The hands are pulled upward, alternately, with short jerking motions. The wool forms a roll.*

Making a Sampler

Before you begin to work, it is advisable to read carefully through this entire chapter.

A good place to make felt is at the kitchen counter. It has an even surface, water and soap are close at hand, and excess water can be discarded easily. Cover the counter with a towel to absorb excess water. Unroll a rush mat on the towel. On top of that put the window screen. To keep your first sample precise, use a waterproof pen to draw a square of, for example, 30 x 30 cm on the screen.

Step 1

Take a piece of carded wool and put it down within the marked area. Place the second piece next to it so that it overlaps the first piece on the left side by 1 cm. The third piece is placed so that it lies under the first one and overlaps the second by 1 cm. The fourth piece covers number three on the left side and number two on the top (fig. 20). Continue this way until the square is completely covered. All pieces are now lying like roof tiles. This is the first layer. The second layer is put down so the wool fibers are lying crosswise to those of the first layer (fig. 21).

Step 2

Before putting down the third and fourth layers, you have to wet the first two layers (fig. 22). Prepare a bottle for the soapy water. A laundry sprinkler or a plant mister will do well, or you can make a sprinkler bottle by punching small holes in an empty plastic soap bottle with a hammer and a small nail.

Dissolve 1 tablespoon olive soap, or soap powder, in a pint of hot water and stir until the soap has completely dissolved. Use a funnel to transfer the soapy water to the sprinkler bottle. Spray the wool carefully, about three times. The suds will lay like little pearls on the surface of the wool. The weight of the moisture will flatten the wool layer somewhat.

For this sample, make four layers. The third layer should lie in the same direction as the first, the fourth in the same direction as the second.

When you now add the third layer, it will adhere slightly to the second layer. When the third layer is in place sprinkle again, lightly, and do the same after the fourth layer.

Step 3

Write down the original measurements of your material, the length and the width, in a small notebook. During the felting process shrinking will occur, and it is important to always record measurements both at the beginning and the end of the process. On future pieces, you will know how much shrinkage to expect. Different kinds of wool will shrink at different rates.

Step 4

The sampler is "wrapped." Fold the screening in half in such a way that it completely surrounds the sampler (fig. 23). Then, using large stitches, baste the piece between the top and bottom layers of screen (fig. 24). Work from the outside edges toward the center to prevent the wool from moving as you sew.

Step 5

The felting can now begin. First sprinkle the piece again a few more times. Or, if you are working with a block of olive soap, rub it once firmly over the screen. Then, with your palms and fingers, press the piece down. Take care that you always work evenly across the whole piece, otherwise an irregular quality of felt will result.

After you have worked the piece for a few minutes, check to see whether you used enough soap and water. The suds should ooze up between your fingers as

20 A square of 30 x 30 cm is drawn on the screen. On it, the first layer of wool is put down like roof tiles.

22

21 The second layer is put down crosswise to the first.

22 The first two layers are sprinkled with hot soapy water.

23 The first sampler is enclosed with screening.

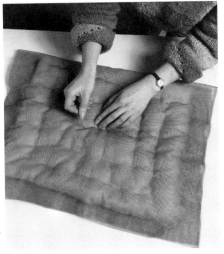

24 With large basting stitches the piece is secured between the top and bottom layers of screen.

you press. Does the soapy water run out between your fingers in little streams? Then it is clear that a little too much has been applied and you will have to press a little longer to reduce the amount of moisture. You also will need to wring out the towel under the rush matting. If no suds appear on the surface when you press, then not enough soapy water was used and you will need to sprinkle the wool again.

Step 6

If all is well, you can begin to rub the piece very carefully. With one or both hands, held flat, make small circles over the piece (fig. 25). It is very important always to rotate the hands in the same direction. Should you rub first to the left and then to the right, nothing will happen.

Remember that the wool fiber has scales, like small barbed hooks, which open up at first contact with hot soapy water, then close again during the continued rubbing process. These small hooks attach to one another when they close, and once the felting process is completed, they are firmly anchored. It is this action that produces the compact material called felt. This is why the wool layers have to be put crosswise on top of each other. This also is the reason you must rotate your hands in the same direction when rubbing the wool.

It is difficult to say how long you should rub. One person may have much stronger hands than another. There may be differences in the way the wool is laid down. For this first sample, try rubbing the wool for twenty minutes. If the wool starts to come through the screen sooner than this you should stop.

Keep a constant watch over the amount of moisture in the wool. When you rub it, the piece loses moisture. Stop once in awhile and test by pressing on the piece. If you can still feel a little moisture between your fingers, everything is all right.

If not, just sprinkle again lightly with soapy water.

It is wise to turn the material over every five minutes and work the other side. After you have rubbed for a total of twenty minutes, remove the basting threads and carefully fold the screen back. Caution is needed because the wool has a tendency to attach itself to the screen.

Step 7

After the screening is removed, the moment has arrived to check whether the piece has turned into "felt." With the nails of your thumb and index finger, take hold of a small amount of wool and carefully pull upward. If the fibers lift up very easily, the felting process is not far enough advanced (fig. 26) and you need to continue rubbing in small circles. You will not need the screening at this point; the wool will no longer stick to your hands and the edges will not change any further.

Step 8

Once the felting procedure has been completed, you will have created a wet woolen material, but it is not yet "hard" enough. The hardening process, during which the material shrinks, is called *fulling*. To begin the fulling, place the rush matting lengthwise in front of you, so that the mat can be rolled toward or away from you. Roll up just a few inches of the mat, then place the piece on the matting just ahead of the roll (fig. 27). Roll the piece in the mat, stopping just beyond the end of the felt piece. It is handy to also roll up the excess matting, so that everything fits nicely on the countertop.

Hold the roll firmly with both hands and work it back and forth as if you were using a rolling pin. The manner in which the roll is worked depends on one's own personal preference.

After five minutes, stop and measure the length and width to see whether any

25 *Rub in small circles, always in the same direction.*

26 *Do the finger test once in awhile.*

27 *Roll the piece in rush matting to do the fulling.*

shrinkage has occurred. During the fulling felt always shrinks in the direction in which it is rolled! If all is well, the piece should by now have shrunk a little in length. Turn the material a quarter turn and roll it again for five minutes. Repeat this action in all directions.

If the sampler was originally 30 x 30 cm, after the fulling it should be about 25 x 25 cm. Shrinkage is usually between 10 and 25%. It is difficult to predict the exact percentage of shrinkage. It depends upon how the wool is carded, the way in which it is laid down and the amount of hand pressure used. You can continue fulling until no further shrinkage takes place, but this is not usually necessary.

With each work piece, keep in mind what its use will be and how firm the material should be. This is the reason samplers are indispensable.

If you have a washboard, you can do the fulling on it instead of rolling the material in the matting (fig. 28). Place the washboard in the sink and rub the material firmly back and forth over the ridges. Watch out—this method works very quickly! Here, too, the rule of continuous turning and changing direction applies.

There are still other ways to full the material. You can wrap it around a broom handle, or you can work it with a rolling pin. It is also possible to do the fulling by walking over the material in your bare feet or while wearing boots (fig. 29). All these methods work; it is for you to find out which is most enjoyable for you.

If you wish to use an ancient, proven technique, try making a new piece of felt on top of an old one, as the nomads did. They called the two pieces of felt "mother and daughter." To make sure that mother and daughter would not felt together, the daughter—the new felt—was turned repeatedly during the process.

Step 9

Do a final check to be sure your work is square by folding the piece diagonally (fig. 30). The edges should align precisely. If this is not the case, you have to stretch the piece in the appropriate direction.

When the material feels firm and has shrunk enough, it is time to rinse it out. Rinse first in warm water, then in cold. It is good for the wool to add a dash of vinegar to the last rinse to neutralize the soap. Squeeze the piece well, and put it back into the form. If you have a board of soft wood you can pin the material to it to dry. Otherwise let it dry flat on a towel, or press it dry with an iron. If you want a napped surface on the felt, this is the time to brush it—in one direction only—with a small, sturdy brush.

If the first piece is a success, try again to get the same results without basting the wool between pieces of screening. Cover the counter with a towel and rush mat, and put the wool directly on the mat. After the last layer of wool is in place and the piece has been sprinkled, put the screening loosely on top for a short period, so you can press down the wool. This will prevent it from sticking to your hands. As soon as the air is pressed from the wool, you can remove the screen. The rest of the process is the same as with the screen, only now you can see and feel everything much better.

If the edges of your material are somewhat thin and ragged, after you remove the screen you can fold over each edge about a centimeter and press it tightly.

Consider this piece as a test. If you are able to felt a nice piece without using the screen, you can move on to other techniques or to a clothing project. If this attempt was unsuccessful, then you should make a third sample, or, who knows? Perhaps a great workshop will soon be offered in your neighborhood....

28 Fulling on a washboard helps achieve a good fit in a garment.

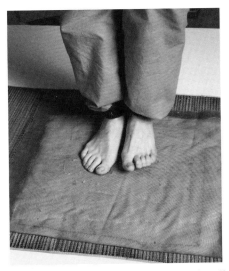

29 Fulling can also be done with your feet. If it's cold, just wear boots!

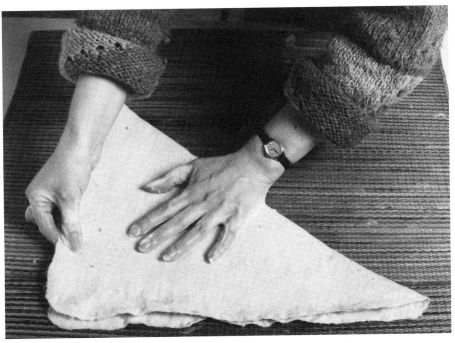

30 Check that the piece is still square by folding opposite corners together.

Felting with Children

When you are working with children it is better to proceed in a slightly different way. The method has to be quicker and more direct; they have to be able to see what they are doing. Plastic boxes, loaf pans, water, soap and wool are the necessary equipment (fig. 31). Here, too, New Zealand batt-carded wool is ideal to use.

Put all the necessary equipment on a plastic-covered table. Let the children choose a pan or box to use as a mold, and give each one a wad of wool.

The child holds his wool in one hand, and with the other pulls small pieces out of the wool and covers the bottom of his mold. Meantime, prepare a spray bottle of hot soapy water. After completing each layer of wool the child can spray it a little. If they use small tufts of short, curly wool it is not as important that they be laid down precisely, or that they are neatly layered like roof tiles. Let the children choose whether they want to make thick or thin felt.

After the layers are in place and have been sprayed, the feltmaking can start. The procedure is slightly different when you use a mold than that used for the first sampler. It's best just to show it. With the fingertips of both hands, press straight down onto the wool. Work all the way around the edge in this manner. If the wool sticks to your fingers, dip them occasionally into warm water.

When the edges have been flattened there will be a "pillow" in the middle of the mold. To flatten it, wet one hand really well and press the center part to the bottom of the mold. Lift the hand very slowly to prevent the wool from sticking to it and pulling up again. Repeat this a few times until the wool remains flat against the bottom of the mold. The edges of the piece will now begin to extend slightly up the sides of the mold. (Remember, the barbed hooks on the wool fibers open then close again during the rubbing process. When they open the piece enlarges, because the wool expands; when it is rubbed, it will become smaller than the mold.)

When all the children have reached this point, check the degree of moisture in their wool pieces. Have them take the wet fleece out of the mold carefully and put it back in upside down. When you notice dry fluff on the bottom of any piece, have the child spray it again with the suds. If water remains in the mold, just have him pour it out. They can then felt for about fifteen minutes using one hand, or the other, or the knuckles or fingertips, whatever they like. Remind them to keep pushing down the outside border with their fingertips.

Once in awhile let them do the finger test, lifting a few fibers with the nails of the thumb and index finger (see fig. 26, page 25). If the fibers come up, it is not ready yet.

When the pieces feel firm enough they can be fulled outside the mold with a rolling pin, on a washboard or in rush matting. The child can also squeeze the piece, or soap it again and wring it out.

Finally the pieces should be rinsed. Then the children can check to see whose piece still fits the mold, and decide what more they want to do with their work. They can decorate with buttons or beads, or perhaps fold it in thirds to make a small neckbag. Most often when a child sees his first piece of felt he immediately has an idea of what it should become.

With children you can also felt marbles and balls. Older children can felt a doll in the washing machine. These instructions are found in chapter V.

31 *Water, wool, and soap for a children's party.*

Dyeing with Steam—
Many Colors in One Bath

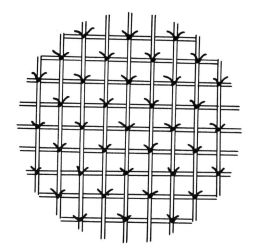

One dyeing method that gives very nice results with felting is dyeing in a steam bath, in which several dye colors can be used at the same time (color plate 2). The advantage of dyeing with steam is that it will not dry out the wool so much.

For the usual dyeing methods, synthetic and vegetable, I refer you to the existing literature on the subject.

For making a dye steam bath you need:

- batt-carded wool, here a little bit of white silk also is used;
- synthetic dye with an acid base;
- household vinegar;
- mordant;
- rubber gloves;
- enamel or stainless steel dye kettle. A rice steamer with a tight-fitting colander is ideal;
- clean glass jars;
- wooden or stainless steel spoons for turning the wool;
- stainless steel teaspoons or plastic spoons to mix the dye;
- scales marked in grams for measuring the dye;
- kitchen scales for the wool.

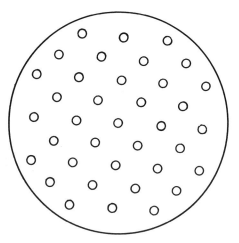

32 Grills of willow and plastic.

Fill the bottom part of the steamer with water and a cup of vinegar. Be sure the bottom of the colander is at least 1cm above the water surface. Put 100 grams of wool in the colander. Here, some silk is dyed along with the wool. There are all sorts of possibilities for mixing fibers. Cover the pan and heat it slowly. The tighter the cover fits, the better the steam can circulate.

Now prepare the dye. Use at least two colors. In this example a solution is made of reddish-purple, red-orange, yellow, and blue dyes, mixed in separate jars. Follow the directions of the recipe, but use a lot less water than the recipe indicates. Here two cups of water were used instead of one liter. Always add an extra dash of vinegar.

When all the colors are mixed and the wool and silk are steaming, pull on your gloves and open the pan. Sprinkle one cup of each color dye on the silk and the wool (color plates 2a, 2b, 2c). Try, for example, pouring the dye over the fibers with a swirling motion, so the dye divides itself over the surface. If one color is poured directly onto another, the colors mix. Yellow over blue becomes green, etc., resulting in a multicolored bath.

After pouring the dyes, quickly cover the pan again and let everything steam for fifteen minutes. If all goes well you will see fantastic patterns formed by the colors.

The wool and silk can now be turned, using dowels or spoons. Check, too, to be sure the water in the bottom of the pan has not evaporated. If necessary, remove the colander and quickly add hot water. After turning the fibers, pour the remaining dyes over the wool, exactly the way you did the first time. Steam it for another fifteen minutes and have another look.

When the result is pleasing, let the wool and the silk steam for an additional half hour. Let the material cool in the pan, then rinse it in water of the same temperature, or let it cool in the colander.

On the bottom of the pan there will be an "exhaust bath," dye which is still useable (color plate 2d). Its color is a blend of all colors used. You can put in a tuft of wool—here 20 grams was used—and perhaps some silk, and dye it according to the standard directions. This way you will acquire an evenly dyed harmonizing color.

If you do not have a rice steamer, or if you want to dye more than 100 grams of wool at a time, you can make a kind of strainer yourself. In the classroom we used an enameled kettle containing two bricks, upon which was placed a grill of willow twigs (fig. 32). You can also make a grill by drilling holes in a piece of hard plastic which has been cut into a circle (fig. 32).

Because many dye recipes work with weights in grams and cubic measures in liters, below is a conversion table to help you:

Weight:	Cubic measure:			
1 kg	= 1000 grams	= 1 l	=	1000 cc (or ml)
	100 grams	= 1 dl	=	100 cc (or ml)
	10 grams	= 1 cl	=	10 cc (or ml)
1 grams	= 1000 mg	= 1 ml	=	1 cc

U.S. liquid measure:
1 oz	= 29.57 cc (or ml)
1 pt	= .0473 l
1 qt	= .946 l
1 gal	= 3.785 l

III. Traditional and Modern Techniques and Motifs

Students in my classes made several samplers exhibiting different technical methods in design of and decoration with felt. A few of these are pictured and discussed in this chapter. There are pieces of work with modern designs, but an equal number feature old motifs such as the cloud, the ramshorn, and the sunwheel (figs. 33 and 34).

The students learned a great deal, too, from the large Pazyryk tapestry (see chapter II). Mosaic technique and applique are used in it, and it is embellished with rich embroidery. Applique allowed the addition of different materials to the tapestries and other felt articles, such as scraps of felt, cotton, silk, metal, even bark and leather.

Felt was sometimes quilted, too. The quilting was done in continuous slanted lines, because a straight line of stitching could split the felt. Figurative designs like flowers, animals, and people were usually embroidered on the felt.

We can assume that many motifs from the early felt tapestries were copied and expanded upon in the woven and knotted tapestries of later periods. In older works can be seen the influence of weaving, knotting and felting in, for example, the geometric motifs and borders.

Felting with Cutout Shapes

Here is a modern adaptation of an age-old theme: the cloud. The cloud is in gold, a symbol of heavenly protection. For this sampler a swirling cloud was drawn (color plate 3e). One piece of felt was made in white, and one in yellow and green. A drawing was pinned to the dyed piece and used as the pattern for cutting. Both the cutout and the piece from which

33 *A variety of old motifs, all depicting the sunwheel.*

it was cut were used as motifs and were stitched onto the white felt. Remember when you do this sample that the background piece has to be twice as large as

34 *Old motifs, such as clouds and ramshorns are still used. The cloud border is also seen on the front cover of this book.*

the piece from which the motif is cut.

This same positive/negative effect can be accomplished by using a different technique. In the picture on page 34 are examples of a geometric form and a small doll (fig. 35). Again two pieces were felted, but in this case the felting was stopped for a short time at an early stage of the process. At the point where the fibers were sprinkled and soaped in, the smallest piece was folded double. The motif was cut out of the folded piece. Here, too, a drawing was used as a cutting pattern. Both the cutout and the piece from which it was cut were put on a larger felt piece and pressed down firmly. The large piece was turned over and the felting process continued. In this way the motifs were felted directly onto the backing.

Feltmaking and Weaving

For this work two pieces were felted, a white one and a soft-colored one. Guidelines were drawn with pencil and ruler. The colored piece was cut into separate strips; the white piece was cut so that the strips could be woven into it (fig. 36). The two pieces were stitched together after weaving.

This technique lends itself to many variations. For example, you can pull tufts out of the wool while it is still dry, interweave them or braid them in, then felt the piece. Or you can felt a piece just through the early stage—the felt is still very soft—then cut it into strips, weave or braid them, and continue the felting process.

35 *Using a cutout form and also using the remainder results in a positive and negative design.*

36 *The top layer is cut, and strips of colored felt are woven through it.*

37 *A variety of different fibers are felted into a sampler.*

Changing Texture and Structure

By layering different materials you can change the structure and texture of the felt. This experiment (fig. 37) was done with a foundation of dark grey New Zealand wool upon which strips of two different fibers were arranged. The diagonal stripes, from bottom right to top left are:

Camel hair (felts well, either alone or mixed with wool; shrinkage is about the same as with wool)

Alpaca (felts well; shrinks much more than does wool)

Swedish wool (felts rapidly; it has the same shrinkage rate as wool)

Icelandic wool (felts well; it shrinks more than wool)

Two colors of karakul (felts well; shrinks somewhat less than other wool)

Ramie is a plant fiber, also called Chinese linen. It attaches well to the wool. Because it does not shrink it will lie in waves.

Linen gives the same result as ramie.

Silk also produces wavy lines, but in more than one direction. Its structure is very fine. (See color plate 3.)

36

a

b

c

d

e

Color plate 3 *Five samplers for which the techniques are explained in chapter III.*

37

Copying a Picture in Felt

To copy a drawing or other picture in felt, first place it in a clear plastic bag. Put the protected drawing on the rush matting, decide upon the appropriate fibers, and you can begin. You will be making the picture upside down—the first layer you place will be the top layer of your felt picture.

The squirrel shown in fig. 38 was laid out using dark brown alpaca and Icelandic wool. It was then sprinkled lightly to keep the fibers in place. The white background was put in place as the second layer and the piece was sprinkled again. Finally two layers of grey New Zealand wool were put on top to create the darker background.

The finished piece will be a mirror image of the original drawing. If this is undesirable, you can trace the drawing first, by taping it against a window and using paper or plastic that is somewhat transparent. When you put the copy in the plastic bag wrong side up, the felted piece will be right side up.

After you have worked for about five minutes on the grey background side of the piece, turn it over and compare the felt drawing with the original. The felt version will always be a free translation. Serious faults can be touched up at this stage with a blunt needle. Then turn the piece over again and work on the back side.

Mixing of Fibers and Colors

To achieve the colors of the tropical fish shown in color plate 3, different colors of dyed wool were mixed with dyed tussah silk, bourette silk, and natural wool. In some cases three colors were mixed to get the desired result. First a sampler was made (color plate 3c), with the colors felted on a layer of white wool and separated by lines of felted yak hair. Colors for the fish were chosen from this series of ten squares.

Accenting with Thread

Here a butterfly is used as an example (color plate 3b). The butterfly shape is composed of old motifs: the ramshorn and the spiral. The spiral appears in nearly every prehistoric culture as decoration on stone statues, on pottery, and even as tattoos. To the early mystics the spiral was an eternity symbol. Here the motif was cut out of a thick piece of felt, then placed on a background piece so the motif stands out in relief. Thread decoration was sewn around the edges of the motif to accentuate the three-dimensional quality.

Cutting Out Designs

For this sample, a layer of white wool, a layer of dyed wool, and another layer of white wool were felted together. The motif—a few triangles—was cut out of the top layer of white wool after the piece was felted and fulled (color plate 3d). Other designs can be worked in this manner too, of course, such as the apple and the pineapple in fig. 39.

38 *A drawing was used as a pattern for a felted picture of a squirrel and his filbert.*

39 *Two or more colored layers can be felted on top of one another, and motifs cut in different ways.*

Applique and Embroidery

The three samplers in fig. 40 were made from three layers of dark grey New Zealand wool. On the top layer white wool was used to make the three stripes and five circles.

On the second sampler an additional circle was embroidered, and the middle stripe was accentuated with a row of darning stitches.

40

The bottom sampler became very lively, because the stripes and circles were covered with fabric. Parts of the stripes were filled in with flannel and embellished with chain stitches. The circles, too, were partially covered with fabric and outlined with back stitches. Small groups of sequins were placed between the circles for a whimsical touch.

Decorating with Sequins and Beads

As you can see in fig. 41, felt lends itself very well to decoration with sequins and small beads. In this sample long basting stitches are applied with copper thread.

Adding Fringe to Felt

Fringe can be laid into the wool before felting. Long, curly sheep's wool or a combination of long and short wool can be used under the wool. To prepare the fringe for felting, pull a curly end out of the tuft. Fluff out the fibers on one end. Continue until you have a supply large enough for your project.

If the fringe is to serve only as a finishing touch along the edges, place the individual pieces, one at a time, on the next to last layer of wool with the fluffed end of tuft inside and the curls outside the edge. When the top layer is in place the fringe attachment will be invisible.

If you want to have fringe all over the surface, as in this example, place the first two layers of wool, then lay a row of fringe all the way across the bottom edge of the piece. Cut a strip of plastic 2-3 cm wide and the length of the piece. Place it so that it covers the very tops of the fringe pieces, where they will attach to the wool. The second row of fringe is put down in such a way that the curly ends lie on the plastic and the fluffed upper ends on the wool, so they will adhere. On top goes another strip of plastic and the process continues.

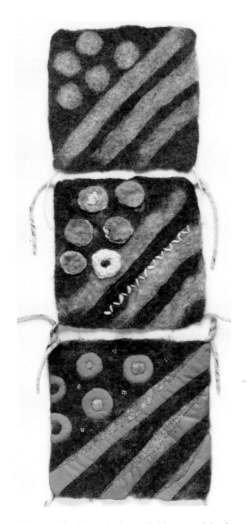

40 In each piece, circles and stripes are felted into the top layer. The center piece was decorated with felt and wool. The bottom one has additional fabric added to highlight the circles and stripes.

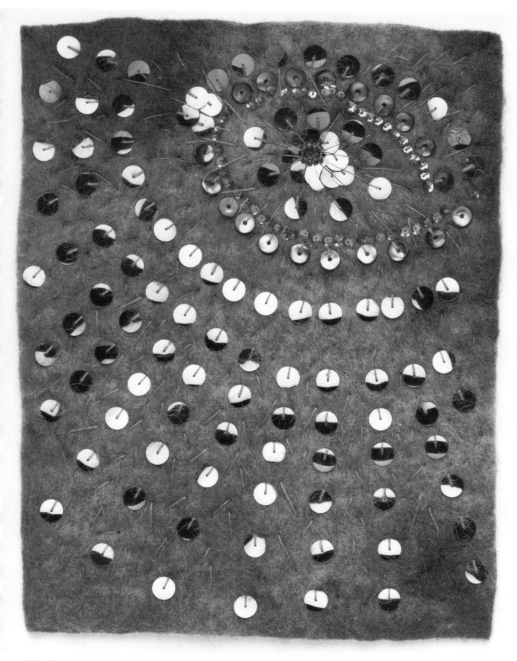

41 *Decorating felt with sequins and copper thread.*

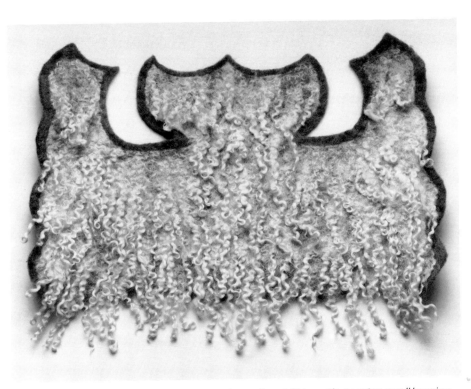

42 *Long curly tufts can be felted in with the top layer of wool. This vest is meant as a wall hanging.*

IV. Clothing

Before you begin to make felted clothing you should have tried the techniques in chapter II and made a few test pieces from chapter III. The only new techniques introduced in this chapter will be those which apply to specific articles of clothing.

The patterns in this chapter are shown as models on graph paper. Your work will be more enjoyable if you first make the pattern to size on large-scale graph paper (i.e. 4x4cm), then trace it onto sturdy, transparent plastic (such as that used for upholstery). The patterns given here are 10 to 20% larger than standard sizes to allow for shrinkage. Of course a purchased sewing pattern is also satisfactory. Choose one with simple lines and few tailoring darts, and buy it two sizes larger than your normal pattern size.

Vest and Coats

The vests shown in color plate 5b were made of just one piece of fabric each. In the blue vest the shoulder seams were felted together. The red vest has inlaid diagonal red and pink stripes. The fringe is felted in (see chapter III); the small feathers were sewn on later. The end of each feather was first wrapped with thread, then the feather was sewn on. The stripes on the blue vest follow the garment's lines; they were laid through all the layers.

For the striped vest in fig. 43 the diagonal stripes are laid into just the top layer of wool. The tulips on the vest at left in the photo were embroidered with chain stitches. This vest is lined, and trimmed with bias tape.

For your first attempt at felted clothing,

43 *The tulips are embroidered with chain stitch. The colored stripes are felted into the top layer of wool.*

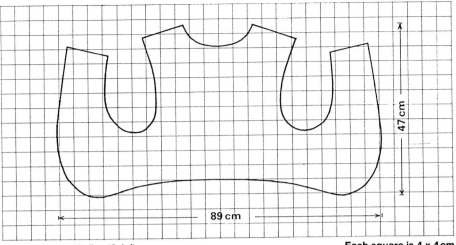

Pattern for vest in fig. 43, left. **Each square is 4 x 4 cm.**

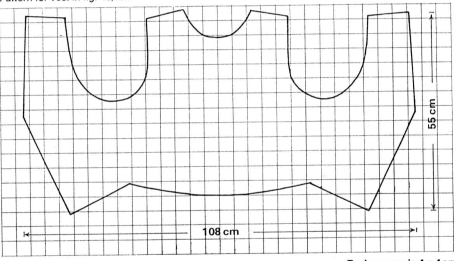

Pattern for vest in fig. 43, right. **Each square is 4 x 4 cm.**

it is best to start simple. Try a plain vest made of three layers of wool. For a vest in size 14 to 16 (European size 40), about 10 or 11 ounces of wool will be needed.

If you want to use a design that incorporates some colored wool, then start with it. Draw guidelines on your pattern with a waterproof pen, and place your pattern on the rush matting. Position the colored wool, then fill in the surrounding area with plain wool.

If you want to work the design into just the top layer, continue with plain wool and put down the second and third layers. Add a fourth layer if you want the vest a little thicker.

The procedure is exactly the same as for the first sampler. Keep the screening

44 *Tulle was cut to the pattern, and the wool layers placed on top of it. Because of its open structure, the tulle felts together tightly with the wool.*

in place only for the first phase. During the fulling process it is best to try on the vest now and then. If there are places that are too large, you can full those a bit longer on the washboard, first pouring a little boiling water over the area. Rub for a longer time in the direction in which you want the felt to shrink.

The jacket with raglan sleeves (fig. 44) consists of two pieces of felted material. A piece of tulle was felted along with the wool. The tulle was cut into shape and placed on top of the plastic pattern on the rush matting. Only two layers of wool were used. The tulle attaches itself to the wool during the felting process, and gives firmness to the felt, so fewer layers of wool are necessary.

The front was made as one piece and later cut down the center. A big plastic separating zipper was sewn in, and decorative machine stitching was added.

It is also possible to felt a backing fabric onto the inside of the garment. A very loosely woven drapery fabric works. Always be sure to take into account the shrinkage rate of the backing material.

A jacket with raglan sleeves is easily made from four rectangular pieces (fig. 45). The advantage here is that you can make four smaller pieces of material—a less tiring process. The design on this jacket consists of simplistic mountains and clouds. The motifs are outlined with thick strands of handspun yarn. The front is made as one piece and later cut. The sleeves are three-quarter length, and the coat comes just to the waist.

Another jacket pattern was adapted to create the raglan pattern. The front pattern piece was laid out, and the sleeve pattern was folded in half, lengthwise, and laid at a right angle in place against the front. The diagonal line of the sleeve

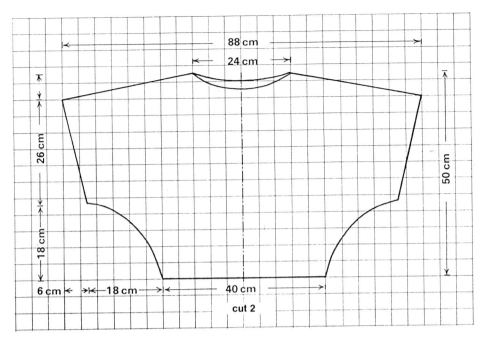

88 cm
24 cm
26 cm
50 cm
18 cm
6 cm
18 cm
40 cm
cut 2

Pattern for the jacket shown in fig. 44.

One square is 4 x 4 cm.

inset comes about by "subtracting" a triangular-shaped section from the front and adding it to the sleeve. The back was done the same way.

The white coat with the red and blue diamond design (color plate 5a) is made just as it might be in a professional felt-maker's workshop. About 25 ounces of wool was used. The coat is made in one piece shaped like a large double T. Four rush mats were sewn together and spread out on tables, with the plastic pattern laid on top. The red and blue patterns were put in place, then six students helped put down the wool for the rest of the coat. That way the work was more pleasant and went quickly. (Of course it is possible to felt a coat by yourself, provided you have plenty of time and space.) When four layers of wool were in place, the wool was sprinkled with hot water, rolled in the rush matting, then rolled back and

forth for ten minutes. When the matting was unrolled the thick wool layer was flattened and had changed into a firm fleece.

Now a second plastic pattern was placed on the wool so the piece could be folded over it, into the coat's T shape, without the front and back felting together. The side seams were felted closed. First the back seam allowance was folded around the plastic pattern, then the back sleeve seam allowance. The front and the sleeve front seam allowances were folded around the folded back seam allowances (there is more about this procedure with the instructions for making hats). The coat was rolled for about half an hour in the rush matting, with hot water sprinkled on the roll occasionally. Only then was soapy water worked into it.

The soaping process resembled an

45 *A jacket with raglan sleeves is made from four pieces.*

old-fashioned laundering. With one hand inside the coat to support the area being rubbed, the soap was worked into the coat one section at a time. Then some firm rubbing took place. The seams were very carefully rubbed first, then the whole piece was once again sprinkled with soap suds. Next the piece was turned, and the back side was worked in the same manner. It was rolled up again, this time around a broom handle instead of in the matting. This step was repeated several times, with the piece rolled in a different direction each time.

Only when the coat had become firm were the neck opening and center front cut open. The coat was tried on then, and fulled a little bit more on the body. Finally the coat was rinsed in hot and cold water alternately, and laid flat to dry. The felt was smoothed with a steam iron—a modern improvement to an old technique. Finally, the seams were trimmed.

Another adaptation of an historic pattern can be found in fig. 46: a modern Hungarian *szur*. This pattern is from a richly embroidered coat like those once worn by farmers and shepherds.

The *szur* was, until this century, an important man's garment. A young man was presented one by his family when he became an adult. The coat was traditional wear for special occasions, such as that of proposing marriage. When the young man left his beloved's home after making his proposal, he would leave his coat behind. If the proposal was accepted, the coat remained at the prospective bride's house; if not, then his *szur* was put out on the steps so he could collect it and make his retreat.

The classical *szur* was often worn as a cape, with the sleeves sewn closed and

46 (right) *A contemporary Hungarian* szur, *now made of machine-felted wool. The decorations, too, are done by machine. The richly ornamented front panels are folded double and meet in back to form a "sailor's collar" that can be folded into a hood.*

48

47 *Even the novice can achieve good results with felted children's clothing.*

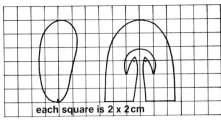

Pattern for baby slippers, fig. 47a

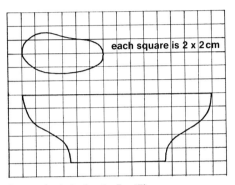

each square is 2 x 2cm

Pattern for baby boots, fig. 47b.

used as bags for transporting the necessities of daily living.

A modern example of felt made by machine is shown in color plate 4. The pattern was laid by hand by London designer Annie Sherburne (see also figs. 49 and 50). She works with the felt manufacturer Bury Cooper Whitehead Ltd. in Lancashire. This gives her the advantage of being able to make large pieces unassisted. While a piece is being produced, she can stop the transport band and apply motifs to the top layer at leisure. She calls the process "painting with wool," because in the making of her woolen paintings she can change her design right up to the last minute. The machine then felts the wool into a firm, even fabric. Her felted pieces are much in demand with, among others, fashion designer Jean Muir, who has them made into short coats.

Children's Clothing

With felted children's clothing, even the novice can achieve good results. The vest at top right in fig. 47 is felted from one piece. The shoulder seams are stitched closed. The technique was previously described in this chapter. Other items of clothing shown here are constructed from pieces of felt. The little coat at top left has knitted sleeves. The front section has a few stripes of colored wool felted into it. It is edged with embroidery. The baby vest has small patches of colored silk felted onto the surface. The slippers are lined for added firmness and as insurance against itching.

Hats

A felt hat can be made by several different methods. You will find in this chapter instructions for a beret and a hat. Each is made as a single piece.

A beret or cap is made from a circle (fig. 49). The diameter of the beret is 30 cm. Cut two pattern pieces out of plastic, and from one of the two circles cut an inner circle with a diameter of 9 cm. This will become the opening of the beret. Weigh out two separate portions of wool, one at 55 grams, and one at 45 grams.

When you are ready to begin, with the counter covered, and all necessities within reach, put the solid plastic circle on the rush matting. Arrange the larger portion of wool in straight rows on the plastic. The wool should extend about 2 cm beyond the pattern edge. Sprinkle lightly after each layer. The donut-shaped pattern piece is now carefully centered on top of the wool layer. Press it down with both hands so the suds underneath will penetrate the wool. The wool that extends beyond the plastic should now be folded inward, over the top piece of plastic.

Arrange the remaining wool, again leaving about 2 cm extending beyond the outer edge of the circle, but keeping the inner circle free. Add an extra layer of

48 *The basic hat pattern can be changed to suit your own taste. On the hat shown upper left, the crown is enlarged so a groove could be pressed into it; the hat at bottom right is stitched in a circular pattern from brim to top. The berets were felted with several different fibers.*

wool just around the inner circle. After the layers are in place and sprinkled, fold the extension back—onto the wool, not against the plastic—and press down for a moment. Cover the beret with screening, sprinkle, and follow the usual procedure (chapter II).

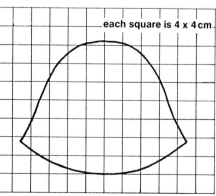

each square is 4 x 4 cm

Pattern for hats shown in fig. 48.

49 *For this triangular hat, a design was worked into the top layer of wool. It was decorated with beads and sequins, and shiny braid encircles the brim.*

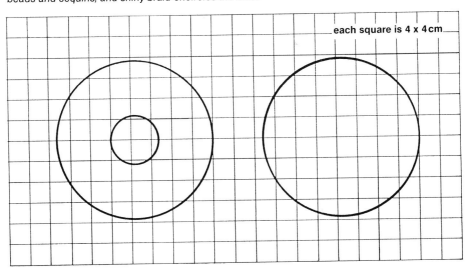

each square is 4 x 4 cm

Pattern for beret (fig. 49).

50 *A wide-brimmed hat cut from material felted by machine. In the background is a piece of machine-made felt 2 x 3 meters. In figs. 49 and 50 are pieces by the progressive English designer and feltmaker Annie Sherburne. See also color plate 4.*

After about fifteen minutes put your hand into the center opening so that the edge "seam" lies across your palm. With your other hand press and flatten the thick folded area. Press until the seam is the same thickness as the rest of the beret. You can use small circular motions to do this, but work very carefully. Remove the plastic before fulling the beret. Fulling can be done either with the beret rolled in the rush matting, or on a washboard.

Only after the beret is rinsed and dried should the opening be cut to size. Do not cut it too soon, though; felt always

stretches a little bit. The inner rim can be reinforced with a grosgrain ribbon, if necessary.

The hat pattern is for a head circumference of 56 cm. The procedure is the same as for the beret. You will need two 50-gram portions of wool. Of course the pattern can be altered to suit your taste. The brim can be widened, or the crown made higher so it can be indented to make a trilby hat.

When you make a hat it is important to make the brim sturdy enough. The instructions will tell you how to do this.

51 *Nothing is warmer than a felted boot. . . .*

Arrange the wool on one of the plastic pattern pieces, adding a seam allowance of 2 cm around all edges of the pattern as for the beret. Sprinkle the wool. Fold the seam allowances under the plastic.

Lay the second pattern on top of the wool. Place the layers of wool on it, adding a seam allowance as you did with the first layers, and sprinkle these layers. Fold the top and side seam allowances under all the layers. Fold the seam allowance at the lower edge of the hat under just the upper plastic piece. After both sides are felted, work on the side seams following the procedure for the beret.

When the whole hat has had its turn, the plastic can be removed. Do this carefully. Put both hands inside the hat. Hold the pattern at the top. Pull it slowly forward and outward. Take care that no fibers adhere to it. Again put both hands inside the hat and fold it so that the side seams lie in the center front and center

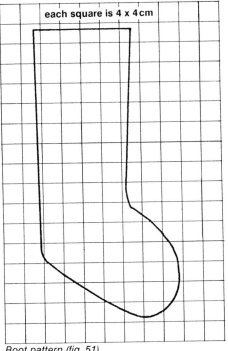

each square is 4 x 4 cm

Boot pattern (fig. 51).

55

Color plate 4 *Two pieces of machine-made felt from English designer Annie Sherburne.*

back. The thickened seams can now be felted away.

The brim should have some additional fulling. Place the hat upright on the rush matting, and rub the brim firmly with both hands. Now try on the hat (you may want to put on a bathing cap first!). If it is too large, full it one more time on the washboard. Rinse it and wring it out, then try it on again. You can adjust it a little further, if necessary, by stretching it carefully. If it fits well, stand it on the mat to dry. The hat is now firm enough that it will stand upright. You can fill the crown with wads of paper so it will retain its shape. For added firmness you can sew grosgrain ribbon to the inside just above the brim.

It is possible, of course, to make a hat from a single piece of felted fabric, from which separate shaped pieces are cut and then sewn together (fig. 50).

Boots and Slippers

There are all sorts of ways to make slippers and boots (fig. 51). The simplest way is to trace the outline of a well-fitting sock or knee sock on plastic, adding 3 cm all around. Notice the position of the foot; it slants slightly downward. In felting, just as in knitting, this gives an excellent fit. The procedure is exactly the same as for a hat or beret. It is recommended that you read through those instructions once again before you begin. For the last fulling it is best to wear the slippers or boots while you rub them firmly with suds. To make a firm sole, put the washboard or the rush matting on the floor and rub your feet firmly over it while wearing the boots.

You can cut soles from a piece of chamois or other leather and glue them to the bottoms of the slippers or boots. With the pair of boots shown at right in fig. 51 a rim was sewn to the leather sole. The sole was glued, and the rim was attached decoratively. Little mirrors were sewn on the instep and around the top edge of each boot.

The boots in the center of the photo have soles which were salvaged from a pair of Yugoslavian ballet shoes. The decoration around the ankles was taken from some worn-out Tibetan boots, and the top border is decorated with a woven ribbon from Staphorst, a village in Holland where traditional costumes are still worn. So your felted boots can be a wonderful experiment in recycling!

Mittens

The difficulty with felted mittens is to make two exactly alike, the same size and the same thickness (see color plate 5a). You can make a pattern yourself. Place your hand flat on a piece of plastic, with fingers together and your thumb as far as possible out to the side. Draw an outline with a waterproof pen, 2 cm away from your hand. Be sure to allow extra length at the wrist. Now cut two pattern pieces for each mitten.

The procedure, again, is the same as for hats. Weigh out two portions of wool, about 30 grams each. If you are making both mittens at the same time, work on one at a time until after the last layer of wool is put down, its seam allowances folded over, and the sprinkling completed. Then work the second mitten to this point. The advantage of making two mittens at the same time is that during the felting process each step can be completed on one of the mittens, then right away on the other. That way they really will be a pair.

Keep in mind that mittens, or any other felt project, once sprinkled and put into its form, can certainly be left overnight, provided the material is covered with plastic to keep it moist.

Bags

The bags pictured (fig. 52) are totally different in appearance, but they are all made the same way: from a single piece of felt. The difference is in the shape and

Color plate 5a *An ensemble in Dutch colors, to keep you toasty warm during the winter. The colored wool is less vivid when it is felted onto white wool.*

5b *Both these vests have inlaid stripes. With the red vest they are diagonal and in the blue vest they are circular, creating a totally different effect. The contrasting stripes are incorporated into all layers.*

Right *Pattern for the coat in color plate 5a.*

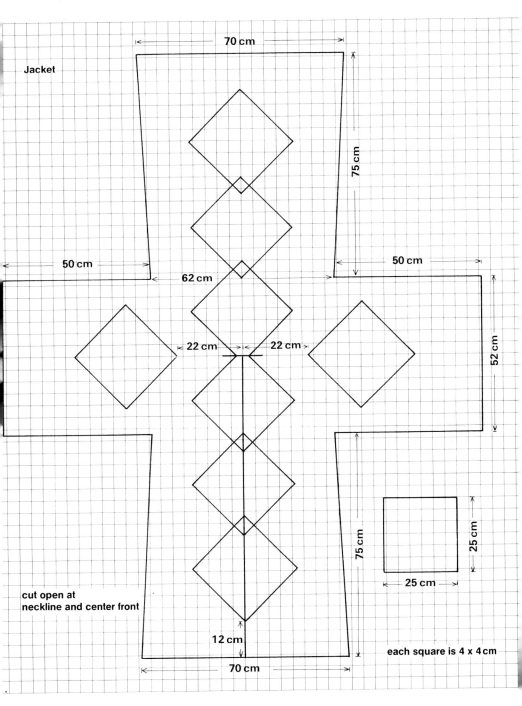

Jacket

70 cm

75 cm

50 cm

62 cm

50 cm

22 cm

22 cm

52 cm

75 cm

25 cm

25 cm

cut open at
neckline and center front

12 cm

70 cm

each square is 4 x 4 cm

59

52 *Bags made from felted samplers.*

the finishing touches. The small polka-dotted case is made from a beginner's first test sample, one that was basted between pieces of screening. It was felted in a washing machine in water of about 140° (60°C).

The little bag at top right in the photo is a felted rectangle of grey alpaca. It was decorated with machine stitching and ribbon, then lined. The bird also was sewn on by machine. Machine stitching on felt produces an odd relief effect.

The bag at bottom left is a piece folded in thirds. The side seams were felted together (for the technique, see the instructions for hats). The decoration was applied as the top layer, of New Zealand wool, was put in place. Alpaca and Icelandic wool in three natural colors were arranged in a pattern of semi-circles. Icelandic and New Zealand wools were spun and twisted into a cord which serves as a shoulder strap.

The large bag in the picture also is made of one piece. The fringe was felted in, as described in chapter III.

V. Other Applications

Marbles, Balls, Beads and Buttons

In addition to its practical application for making clothing, felting is a good technique for creating three-dimensional forms. Marbles are one example. Making them is a pleasant and relaxing task, and one which children love, too.

Cover a table with plastic and have a small bowl of hot soapy water ready. You can use any kind of wool: scraps of different colors, sliver, and carded or uncarded wool. Sliver is best divided first into strips of about 20 cm. The same applies to wool that has been carded on the drum carder (see chapter II). If you are using carded rolag you can pull out thin pieces of the length you need. Uncarded wool must be loosened well at the tips, with your fingers or with a small iron comb.

Hold a strip of wool in one hand and wrap it twice around the index and middle fingers of the other hand. Remove the wrap from the fingers and dip it briefly into soapy water. Squeeze it out well. Then hold the wet tuft between your thumb and index finger and wrap dry wool around it twice. Pinch it firmly, so the suds inside penetrates through the dry outer layer. Turn the tuft a quarter turn and squeeze again. If no moisture comes through the wool, dip it and squeeze it again. Continue the process of wrapping with wool, squeezing, turning, and soaping. After about ten repeats you will have in your hand a wet wad with no resemblance to a marble. Do not let this discourage you. Just a few more minutes' effort will make the wad firmer. Now put the wad in the palm of one hand, cover it with the other, and carefully try to roll it into a small ball. If you are successful, increase the pressure and roll a firm small ball. If you want to make more marbles at this time, you can put this one aside until the others are ready, and rinse them all at once.

You can make the marbles flat or make them elliptical. Toward the end of the process put them on the table and flatten

53 *A ball can be made by felting around a "real" ball.*

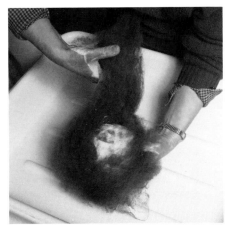

54 *Divide the wool into strips, each long enough to surround the ball.*

61

55 *Sprinkle the wool until it is well moistened.*

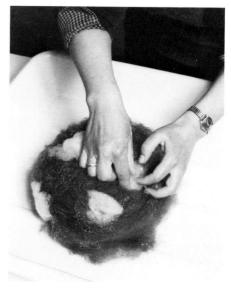

56 *A polka dot design was applied to the top layer.*

57 *Hold the ball between your hands and compress the wool over the entire surface.*

58 *Be patient. The wool will soon begin to shrink and the outer ball will fit around the inner one like a second skin.*

them with your hand. Shaped this way they can be used as beads or as buttons (color plate 6).

Balls

Once you have made a few marbles, then making balls by the same method will not give you any problem. It is just a matter of making marbles that are bigger around. As the ball becomes larger it is no longer necessary to work with strips of wool. It is more effective to use carded sliver. Then at each step you can cover the entire surface with dry wool, which will make the ball easier to shape.

Another way to make a ball is by felting over a tennis ball or a rubber ball (fig. 53). With this method it is best to work in a dishpan or at the sink so you can dispose of the excess water easily.

Divide the wool into strips, each long enough to surround the ball (fig. 54). Start by wrapping once, then turn the ball a little, wrap again, and repeat a third time if necessary. Sprinkle the wool until it is well moistened (fig. 55). Wrap the whole ball again, sprinkle, and so on. Make the wool layer about 1 cm thick. You can add some decoration to the top layer, if you wish (fig. 56).

After the final sprinkling with suds compress the entire surface of the ball between your hands (fig. 57). Because the wool fiber will expand at first, it will seem that you have worked too loosely, but that is not the case. If you calmly continue felting, and perhaps rub the surface in small circles (always in the same direction), the wool will start to shrink (fig. 58). After about fifteen minutes the wool will fit around the ball like a second skin.

You can full a felted ball with your hands on a washboard, or in a washing machine. For this procedure, see the instructions for dolls and mice.

Dolls and Mice

With just a few snips of the scissors a felt ball can become a doll's head. In fig. 59 you see an Indian. His head is cut from a felt ball and his hands are cut from two halves of a ball. The first time you make a doll's head it will be difficult to predetermine how it will look. The first head is usually one of which you will say "It is supposed to be a. . . ." The first arms and legs you make will probably need some adjustment, too. After some practice it becomes easier to predetermine your results. The gnome in the photo is the result of much experimentation. To get the desired skin color, dye tests were done and many different carding mixtures were tried.

The best time to start cutting the doll's features (see the cutting diagram, page 65) is after the ball has become firm but before the soap has been rinsed out. For the ears, make two small vertical cuts on opposite sides of the ball, in the center. Put the point of the scissors straight into the felt, about 1 cm above the midway point. Make the cut about ½ cm deep and 2 cm in length (for a head no larger than a tennis ball). Take the head between your hands and with your thumbs push in the cut on the front side. With your index and middle fingers, rub the back side of the cut toward the front. If necessary, use more soap suds during the rubbing.

To make eyes—or rather orbits—make two horizontal cuts about 1½ cm wide and 1 cm deep on the front, even with the tops of the ears. Now hold the head in one hand and push in the underside of the cut with the thumb of your other hand. With your middle and index fingers rub the upper side of the cut (the eyebrow) to the front. Use more soapy water if necessary. You can carefully round off the lower edge of the cut with scissors to get

59 *The Indian's head and hands are cut from a felt ball. The gnome is felted in the washing machine. The mice are cut from one piece of felt.*

ear   cut 2

upper side
cut 2

underside
cut 1

each square is 2 x 2 cm

Pattern for the mice in fig. 59.

a nice transition to the cheeks.

For the mouth make a shallow horizontal cut even with the bottoms of the ears. You can push the cut into the desired shape: mouth corners up for a happy face, mouth corners down for a sad face, and so on.

Cutting the nose is the most difficult. Cut two lines, starting 1 cm under the inner eye corner and slanting toward the outer corner of the mouth. Start with a shallow cut, then gradually push the scissors deeper into the felt. Stop at least 1 cm above the mouth corner. After cutting lines for the nose put the head on a table and push the cuts downward on both sides of the nose. Now make a small horizontal cut under the nose. This one will automatically stick out.

60 *Cutting diagrams for faces and hands.*

Shape the head further by using sculpting motions and more hot soapy water.

The Indian in the picture wears braids of unspun flax. His little coat is fitted to each wrist, with the head fastened directly to the coat front. A hole was cut in the underside of the head, into which two fingers just fit. So the Indian is a puppet!

65

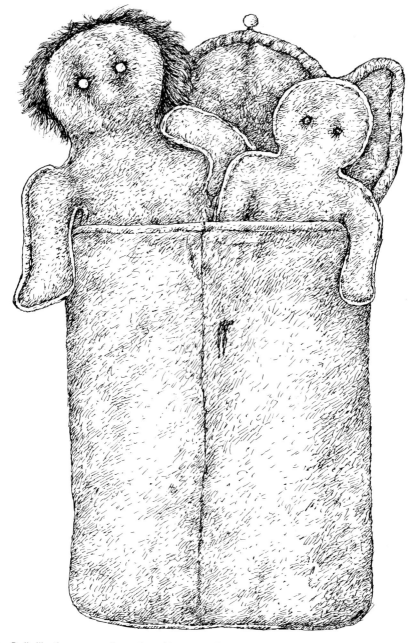

61 *Dolls like these were always found in nomads' tents. They were attributed with magic powers.*

Color plate 6 *A freestyle form that was felted around a ball, and a selection of felt balls. All pieces were dyed with synthetic dyes after the felting.*

67

The rounded hands are made from a ball cut in half. The rounded side becomes the back of the hand. With four cuts you suggest a thumb and fingers. The other hand is cut in mirror image. Cut the thumbs a little thicker than the fingers. With hot suds you can rub the hands into the desired shape.

The mice in fig. 59 are easily made from a piece of felt. Copy the patterns on transparent plastic, cut them out of felt, and put them together. Many different kinds of dolls and animals can be made in this manner.

In fig. 61 you see an example of dolls from the Nomadic period. These two dolls were simple shapes cut from a single layer of thick felt. Dolls like these were found in every tent, and were attributed with magic powers.

Felting in a Washing Machine

A washing machine can be used as a fast felter. The disadvantage is that it is just about impossible to control the felting process. The wool must be basted tightly between pieces of screening (see chapter II), otherwise too much shrinkage will occur. Shrinkage is the greatest, of course, with hot water, and the least with a water temperature of 68-86°F (20-30°C). Because every washer is different, it is always best to make samples at different water temperature settings.

With colored wool you cannot use soap or detergent that contains bleach.

The washing machine is especially handy when you want to make, for example, a whole series of balls, and the shrinkage rate is unimportant. You will need an old pair of panty hose or stockings. Use ones without runs, for runs will cause the felt to be lumpy. Cut off the panty part and the feet, and knot one end. Prepare the wool as for forming balls. Work without suds, but simply keep winding dry wool. It must be wound rather tightly. After finishing a ball, put it in the stocking. Tie a knot above each ball, as close to it as possible.

Dolls, too, can be felted in a washing machine. All the limbs will fit together in one leg of a stocking.

A thin stick, such as a wooden skewer, is useful for forming arms and legs. Wind colored strips of wool tightly around the sticks. Make the arms a bit shorter than the legs, and a bit thinner. In fig. 62 you can see that the arms, after they are pushed off the stick, are put into the stocking next to one another. Sew through the stocking with large basting stitches to keep the arms separated. Knot the stocking close to them. Put the legs into the stocking in the same way. When you make the doll's body, it is best to use a somewhat thicker stick, a pencil, for example. The body requires about three times the amount of wool as does an arm or a leg.

When the stocking is filled, pour boiling water over it before it goes into the washing machine to start the shrinking process. In fig. 63 you can see how the doll will emerge from the washer. At this point facial features can be cut into the head as described previously.

Freestyle Felting and Stiffened Felt

A few examples of freestyle work with felt and hardened felt are discussed below: a hollow and/or a rounded form and a folded form. In color plate 8 are four hardened felt forms. They are simply decorative forms, meant to be enjoyed. The rounded form was felted around a rubber ball, then cut (fig. 64).

Just when the wool begins to fit as tightly as a skin around the ball, and before the soap is rinsed out, start at a central point and cut a few lines with scissors. On the ball shown in the photo, the cut lines are equidistant and even in length (fig. 65). That is a matter of preference. You can let your imagination guide you (fig. 66).

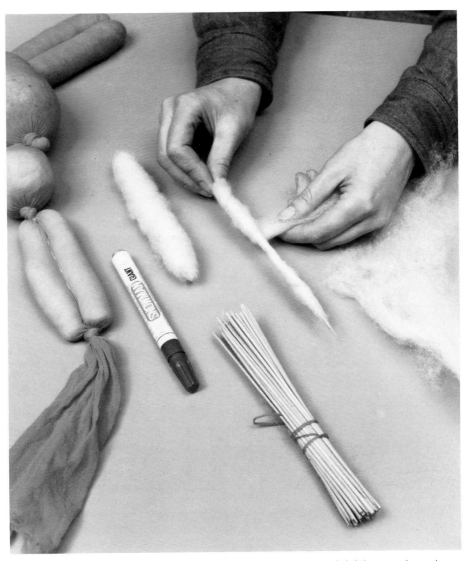

62 For a doll's arms and legs, wool is pulled into strips and wound tightly around wooden skewers.

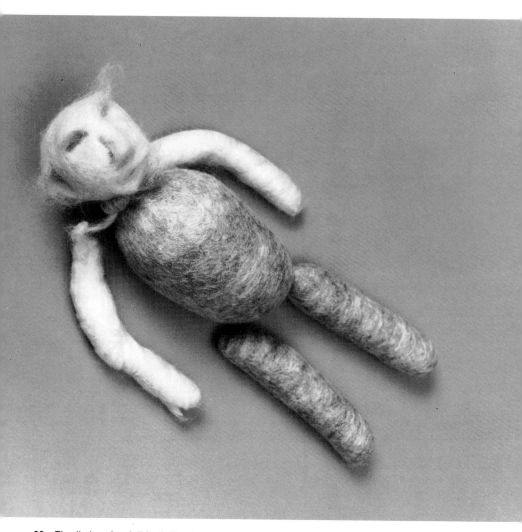

63 The limbs of a doll look like this when they come out of the washing machine. The facial features have been cut and fashioned, but still need further molding with hot soapy water.

64 Two layers of white wool, with accents of black Icelandic wool, are felted around a ball.

65 The ball will be removed to make a free form. Two lines of equal length were cut.

66 When the felt is folded open you can see the symmetrical cuts.

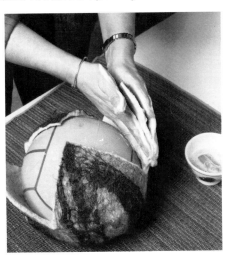

67 The cut edges are fulled once again before the ball is removed.

71

68 *Bone glue is warmed in a double boiler or over a pan of hot water.*

69 *The ball is submerged in the glue.*

After the lines are cut, the cuts are sprinkled with hot suds and fulled once again (fig. 67). Then the ball can be removed, and the hollow, rounded form can be rinsed.

Bone glue, a natural product, is used as a stiffener. Other methods of stiffening are available, but are not discussed here. The procedure is simple and the glue is pleasant to work with. Afterward, the glue can be washed off your hands with water and soap.

For a globe form made with 20 grams of wool, weigh out 10 grams of bone glue. Put the glue in the top of a double boiler or other small pan and add to it three times the wool weight in water. Heat the mixture over a pan of water (fig. 68).

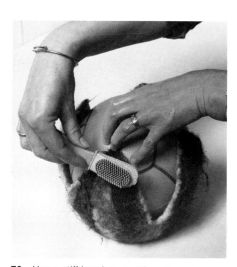

70 *Use a stiff brush to roughen the surface.*

When the water in the bottom pan begins to boil, turn the heat to low. The mixture will look cloudy now. Stir it with a wooden spoon until it becomes syrupy, and the glue is ready.

Put the pan of glue on the counter and submerge the felt in it (fig. 69). Press the felt well into the liquid, squeeze it out, and immerse it again. The glue will be totally absorbed into the wool. Replace the felt around the ball to make a continuous round form. You can, if you wish, roughen the surface of the felt with a small firm brush (fig. 70). Then remove the ball again and let the globe dry.

At the left in figs. 64 through 66 is a square folded form. It was made from a piece of white felt with a colored top layer. This piece was felted and glued, and placed on the plastic-covered counter with the colored side down. The four corners were folded to the center one at a time. The borders were worked from the inside outward with a small steel brush. This caused them to curl somewhat, so the white inside layer became visible.

If you like the idea of molding stiffened forms like these, try to duplicate these two shapes. Or simply let them inspire you. That was the idea behind the intention of the four forms in the series "My Cape is My Castle." The inspiration for the creation of these capes came from the fascinating history of feltmaking, from the time when the shepherd's cape was also a portable tent, his only shelter during bad weather (fig. 71).

71 *The shepherd's cape was also a portable tent, a shelter during bad weather. His hat is made in such a way that it is practical both in summer and in winter. In winter he could pull the brim down over his ears; in summer he turned the hat so that the brim became a sunshade.*

74

VI. Group Feltmaking

Felting a Blanket the Old Nomadic Way

With a group of pupils who understood the basic technique well, a plan was conceived to felt something big. We thought about Noah, who built his ark just before the flood. According to tradition he covered the deck with loose sheep's wool before he let the animals inside.

After forty days the ark had a wall-to-wall carpet of felt.

Next we thought about the nomads. In groups of men or of women, they made all the felt they needed for daily living. We also studied their methods. We decided to follow the old ways of working as closely as we could. We gave up working

72 *The clouds are finished and the waves have their turn.*

73 *Work sessions were very intense.*

74 *Fulling the background with New Zealand wool which had not been presoaked with soapy water.*

on the floor. In place of desert sand or a marble floor we chose a large table as work site.

We wanted to make blankets, blankets to hang on walls or to cover beds, and rugs for tables or for the floor. We let the dice decide which person's project we would work on. The chosen one provided his own design, and the whole group helped him determine the technique, the size, the function and the colors. The felting took one to two days, with about ten people working at it.

The photo sequence shows the felting of a blanket. It is also shown on the cover of this book. Our other group projects include the wall hanging with the fans pictured on page 6, and the blanket with the rosette (color plate 1, the frontispiece). The blanket described on these pages has a cloud and wave border design, an age-old theme (fig. 34, page 33). The reverse side also was designed in accordance with nomadic tradition, with a simple pattern of circles on a white background.

The person for whom the blanket was felted prepared the wool for felting. In this case New Zealand wool was used, dyed with plant dyes in shades of pink and green, then pulled into strips. Many pieces of rush matting were sewed together and the design sketched on it with waterproof pen.

The morning the project began, we started with wetting and soaping the matting. Then each felter received a portion of wool and started to put it in place. In fig. 72 the cloud pattern is finished and we are at work on the wave design, pushing the waves into position with the help of a little soap and water (see also color picture 7a). Fig. 73 shows how hard everyone is concentrating.

After the pattern was put down, we filled in the background, also of New Zealand wool. This wool was not presoaked with suds (fig. 74). The close-up photo shows plainly how the wool was pulled out (fig. 75). The person who volunteered to work in the center had a very difficult time because of the limited amount of

a

b

c

d

Color plate 7 *The felting process in full swing.*

space for movement (fig. 76). Color plate 7b shows that she was successful.

The waves were checked once again for shape. They could differ from one another as long as they expressed a nice, even motion (fig. 77). Next the white wool was sprinkled. Then everyone backed away to give the piece a critical look from a distance (color plate 7c).

Two layers of white wool were put in place. Slowly the clouds and waves of the design disappeared under a thick, white covering of fiber (color plate 7d). The second and third layers were placed with the fibers going in different directions (which can be seen in fig. 78), and these layers were sprinkled.

The reverse side was patterned with

circles and was given a wide, green border. In fig. 79 you can see how thick the fibers were with all the wool layers in place.

The whole blanket was covered with screening. Considerable sprinkling was done, and bars of soap were rubbed over the screen. Then the air was pressed out of the wool (fig. 80).

Only after the completed blanket was laid flat on a table could the screen be removed. The creases indicate how the wool fiber had expanded in these moist conditions (fig. 81).

Now the blanket was felted, a little at a time. The felters pushed with wet, soapy hands, very gently at first, then more firmly.

When the entire blanket had been treated, it was rolled in rush matting (fig. 82). The excess suds drained off.

Slowly but surely the wool became a firm piece of fabric. After much rhythmical movement, unrolling the blanket, turning, and rolling it again (fig. 83), we finally unrolled the matting to find felt!

The next day, to make the felt somewhat firmer, we walked all over it with our boots on. After a few hours of walking the blanket was firm enough to be taken home. It was rinsed under the shower, and hung over a household ladder to dry.

When the blanket was dry, it was pressed completely, with a cloth dipped in vinegar water.

Once again we had made a blanket that was more beautiful than all its predecessors, and that always makes us look to the next one with great anticipation.

75 *A close-up clearly shows how the wool was pulled out.*

76 *The person in the center had little freedom of movement.*

77 *The shapes could differ from one another as long as they conveyed a continuous sense of motion.*

78 *The second and the third layers were laid in different directions.*

79

Color plate 8 *Four forms of hardened felt, from the series "My Cape is my Castle."*

79 Notice the thickness of the blanket with all the layers of wool in place.

80 The blanket was covered with screening, sprinkled with soapy water, and the air pressed out. Then it was rubbed.

81 The creases show how the wool fiber expanded under these moist conditions.

82 *After the felting, the blanket was rolled in rush matting.*

82

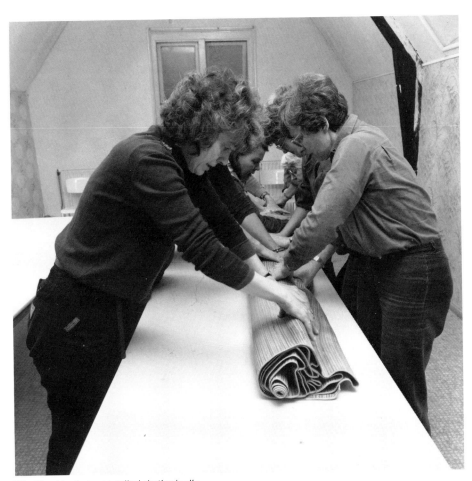

83 *The blanket was rolled rhythmically.*

Additional Reading

Books:
Burkett, M. E. *The Art of the Feltmaker*
Abbot Hall Art Gallery
Kendal, Cumbria 1979

Fannin, A. *Handspinning*
Van Nostrand Reinhold
New York 1970

Gervers, V. *The Hungarian Szur*
Royal Ontario Museum
Toronto 1973

Gordon, B. *Feltmaking*
Watson-Guptill Publications
New York 1980

Green, L. *Feltmaking for the Fiber Artist*
Greentree Ranch Wools
Loveland, Colorado 1978

Levine, L. D. *Notes on Feltmaking and the Production of Other Textiles at Seh Gabi, a Kurdish Village*
from: Studies in Textile History, V. Gervers, Royal Ontario Museum, Toronto 1977

Michaud, R. and S. *Caravans to Tartary*
Viking Press
New York 1978

Articles:
Ciba Review 129 *Felt*, CIBA Ltd, Basel Switzerland Nov. 1958

Shuttle, Spindle and Dyepot, spring 1976, winter 1979, spring 1980.

Fiberarts, July/Aug 1986

Sources of Feltmaking Supplies

The suppliers listed here offer a variety of wools and other fibers, dyes, and carding equipment suitable for feltmaking. Most of them will send samples for a small charge. Write or telephone for prices and current stock availability.

North America

AUTUMN HOUSE FARM
R.D. 1, Box 105
Rochester Mills, PA 15771
(412) 286-9596

CREEK WATER WOOL WORKS
P.O. Box 716
Salem, OR 97308
(503) 585-3302

THE FIBER STUDIO
P.O. Box 637, Foster Hill Road
Henniker, NH 03242
(603) 428-7830

PATRICK GREEN CARDERS, LTD.
48793 Chilliwack Lake Road
Sardis, BC V2R 2P1 Canada
Wool pickers and carding equipment only

RIVER FARM
Route 1, Box 401
Timberville, VA 22853
(800) USA-WOOL
(703) 896-9931 in VA, AK

WILDE YARNS
P.O. Box 4662, 3737 Main Street
Philadelphia, PA 19127-0662
(215) 482-8800

YARN BARN
Box 334
918 Massachusetts Street
Lawrence, KS 66044
(800) 468-0035
(913) 842-4333 in KS

England

FIBRECRAFT STYLE COTTAGE
Lower Eashing
Godalming, Surrey GU7 2QD

FRANK HERRING
High Street
Dorchester, Dorset

LITTLE LONDON SPINNERS
Unit 8, Home Farm Workshop
East Tytherley Road
Lockerley, Romsey
Hampshire S0F1 0JT

MOORVIEW TEXSTYLES LTD.
P.O. Box 23
Rochdale 0L11 5JN

SHETLAND FLEECES
Rosemary Bridgeman, Secretary, S.S.B.G.
33 Pickwick
Corsham, Wiltshire

ADELAIDE WALKER
Regina Mills, Gibson Street
Bradford BD3 9TT

WINGHAM WOOLWORKS
Old Building Yard
Rotherham, South Yorkshire

YARNCRAFT
Three Ply House
57A Lant Street
London SE1 1QN

Readers may be interested in contacting
The Feltmakers' Association
Ewa Kuniczak-Coles, Secretary
5 Harold Rd., Hayling Island, Hampshire
The association was founded in 1985, and issues a quarterly newsletter.

Credits

Most of the works shown in this book were made by students of Inge Evers. They are as follows:

Lenie van Amstel: figs. 37, 38; center and upper left pieces in color plate 3.
Ans Brandhof: figs. 40 bottom, 47 center.
Anneke Bonestroo: fig. 47 bottom left.
Iet Hocker: fig. 47 top left.
Ineke Hoekstra: fig. 2 bottom right.
Maaike van Huizen: fig. 35 bottom, 47 top right, 48 top, 52 top left, color plate 5b bottom.
Murillo Ket: fig. 31 top center.
Frans Kessler: fig. 48 center right.
Elly Leemshuis: frontispiece, fig. 40 center, 48 center left, 52 bottom left, color plate 6.
Hennie van Liemt: fig. 47 bottom; color plate 3 bottom left and right.
Anneke Mantje: figs. 36, 47 slippers, 51 right, color plate 10, fig. 30 top right.
Paula Moison: fig. 43 left.
Ans Roeland: fig. 39.
Gre Schrijver: fig. 47 bottom.
Annie Tukker: fig. 31 top left.
Ad Westen: fig. 35 top.
Nels Wierda: fig. 43 right, 47 top right, and center.
Barbel Wolf: fig. 31 top right.

Work not otherwise credited is by the author.

Special thanks go to Wyke Evers, Marjolein Folmer and Hennie van Liemt, who read the text critically, and to the students who spent their own time photographing the different processes: Willem Evers, Murillo Ket, Elly Leemhuis, Anneke Mantje, Paula Moison, Nels Wierda and Barbel Wolf.
Also a special thank-you to Peter Andrews for the prevention of an error that was made many times; to Mary Burkett, who allowed us to use the cover photograph (fig. 4) from her own book (see bibliography); to Peter Collingwood for supplying literature and other information and to the Stichting J. H. V. U. in Haarlem for allowing us the use of a classroom for photography.

Credits for the Drawings of Ger Daniels

Fig. 2a, 2d: S.I. Ivanov—Materialy po izobkazitel. Nomu iskusstvu naropov sibiri XIX Nacala IIv. Trudy instituta etnografii N.S. Bd Leningrad 1954
2a: page 324, *2d:* page 330
Fig. 2b, 2c: Mikhail Gryzanov—Siberie du Sud Nagel—Geneve 1969
2b: page 132 Petit tapis de selle. Altay, Pazyryk 5e-6e eeuw v. Chr.
2c: page 119 Reconstruction d'ornement de harnais Altay, Pazyryk I, 5e-6e eeuw v. Chr.
Fig. 3: Art of the World
Art of the Steppes—K. Jettmar
Methuen—London 1967
F. P. 1964 Baden—Baden, Holle Verslag G. M. B. H.
Picture 100: Appliqued felt swan intended as decoration for a funeral wagon.
Fig. 5: Atlantis—Heft, juli 1929.
Page 420
Photo: W. Bossard
Chinees Turkestan 1929, Vilten Kirgiezen tent with felt entrance.
Figs. 6, 6a: Karutz—Die Volker Asiens
Fig. 6b: Caravans to Tartary—R. and S. Michaud, Chene—Paris 1977

Fig. 21: Color photo (detail) Kirgiezen Afganistan, in the seventies
Picture 8: Studies in textile history—Veronika Gevers Rom. Toronto, Canada 1977
The Rise and Spread of Old World Cotton—A. M. Watson
"Carding the raw cotton with a bow" illustration in a Persian manuscript 'Muftah al-Fuzala' by Muhammad 6. Da'us 6. Muhammad Shadiyabad i, probably late 15th century. British Library. Oriental manuscripts OR 3299 London
Fig. 33a: see fig. 3b
Pictures 34, 35, 36
Fig. 33b: see fig. 2b
Picture 117, 118: Chabraque laine, Altay—Pazyryk
Fig. 34: see fig. 2a
Page 644, picture 86, 87
Fig. 61: Rolf Gilsberg—Den fener—haeggede en mongolisk Shaman Pose med filtdukker
Fig. 71: 'The Quashqa' i of Iran—World of Islam Festival 1976
Whitworth Art Gallery. University of Manchester
Photo picture 16: Sheperd
Photography: Peter Wallum